I Am Woman

The Empowerment and Transformation of Women

Victoria Howard
with
Allan Jay Friedman

authorHOUSE®

AuthorHouse™
1663 Liberty Drive
Bloomington, IN 47403
www.authorhouse.com
Phone: 1-800-839-8640

First published by AuthorHouse 8/11/2011

ISBN: 978-1-4634-3297-3 (e)
ISBN: 978-1-4634-3299-7 (sc)

Library of Congress Control Number: 2011912112

Printed in the United States of America

Introduction

First, I want to say that I am not a psychologist and do not have all the answers. I am just a normal woman, like you, who has gone through many different chapters in my life.

This is not my story—it is ours. I was born into an Italian, Catholic family and was adored by my parents. I, like 60 percent of children today, had parents who divorced, leaving me in a tug-of-war between two adults who fought for my attention, thus overindulging and spoiling me.

After my parents divorced, my father would spend Sundays with me when he was in town. He was a musician and was on the road a lot of the time. Poor dad didn't know what to do with a five-year-old child, so he shoved me onto his family. I was like a hot potato, tossed here and there.

I was blessed by God with an unbelievably exciting and gifted life. I was a model, dancer, racehorse trainer, beauty queen, and co-owned automobile dealerships.

You might say that I had everything, but there was an emptiness, a void inside me, that left me feeling lonely, and unhappy.

I married my childhood sweetheart and had a beautiful son by him. I thank God for that. I guess I married too early (or maybe I was just too immature), for my marriage ended ten years later.

Thus, the pattern in my life began. I swore I would never divorce and do to my child what my parents had done to me, but I did. Many years later, I married a much older man I had known for several years. He was my best friend and I loved him dearly. It was not until years later that I discovered he was bipolar. That's when the roller-coaster ride began.

The ups and downs, the fear of saying the wrong thing or giving the wrong kind of look, was an everyday occurrence. I lived like I was walking on eggshells, but I still loved him. (Or perhaps I just loved the idea of being in love.)

My husband told me what to wear and who my friends would be and would criticize me if I gained a pound or two. When I think about this today, I am angry at myself for allowing him to do this to me. I don't blame him. I blame myself for allowing this and for not taking responsibility for my own decisions and my own life.

Again, I didn't want to go through another divorce because my son had adjusted to the new place where we had moved, his new friends, and school.

When I was thirty-six, I was a contestant in the Mrs. USA Pageant. When I didn't come in first place, my husband wanted a divorce. He said he was "ashamed to go back to our State with a loser." Now, years later, I see that I wasn't the loser … he was!

Unfortunately, at the time, I didn't realize what had happened to me. I had lost my identity, and all perception of who I was.

It appeared that I never made the same mistake just once. Where was the person my friends and employees called Sunshine, because I was always smiling? I was the real-life Stepford Wife, walking and talking and looking pretty. But I was a scared, lifeless, and soul-less woman (or a poor excuse for one) trapped inside a body, who put on a "happy mask" and hid her problems from both family and friends.

After years of therapy, I got the courage to leave my husband and move away. It was then that I rediscovered myself and learned to like myself again. I had always done everything for everyone, never, ever putting myself first.

The day I left my husband, his last words were that I would "never be anything without [him]."

I didn't know it at the time, but his telling me that gave me the courage and strength I needed to do what I was meant to do: help other women transform themselves and empower them to be what they were meant to be—free and independent.

So, you see, I am no different from you, perhaps just a little better role model because of my experiences and painful awareness. Because of this, I may be better able to show other women that if I could walk away from the lifestyle of the "rich and famous" to which I was accustomed, they can as well.

I finally learned that our self-worth and self-love is

much more important than all the money, glitz, and fame in the world, because that doesn't buy you true happiness, unconditional love, or a place in heaven.

After my divorce I took a trip to Australia with a spiritual group of people from all walks of life. There were doctors, judges, writers, and housewives. While touring an Aboriginal village, an American translator told me that the chief of the tribe asked if I would take off my sunglasses.

When I did, the chief told the translator that he would like me to stay with his people in their village for a few days because I was a "very old soul." At first, I was unsure and afraid, but the other people in the group convinced me that not only was this all right and safe but an honor.

I told the translator I didn't have my toothbrush, clothes, or makeup with me. She laughed and said I wouldn't need them.

I cannot tell you what those three magical days were like with these amazing people in the Outback. Although there was no verbal contact, I didn't need it. I saw how they prepared their food, and watched the children play, the women paint, and the men hunt for dinner.

Those three days were the happiest and most peaceful days in my entire life. I didn't want to leave when my group came back for me. But I had a son and a wonderful mother in the United States who were patiently awaiting my return. Obligingly, I returned to America, but only after saying my good-byes to my new friends, who will always be in my heart.

As I left, the translator told me that the chief had said there was something very big I had to do. When I asked what it was, she replied, "When the time is right, you will know."

When I returned to America, I felt a strange, new peace that I had never felt before.

I have been divorced since 1998, by my choice. I was engaged twice, but finally, I was able to see that old pattern of mine starting to rear its ugly head again. I had made my last mistake, I hoped.

It is only in the past few years that I have discovered that I really like who I am—even with wrinkles and an inch or two to pinch.

I wrote a book called *Why Women Love Bad Boys,* to which many women related. They started asking me how to stop this dysfunctional pattern of choosing the wrong type of man. And believe me, I knew!

The media called me, "The Bad Boy Expert." That, I truly was, because I had experienced almost every bad guy in good guy's clothes that you could imagine. The truth is, I would much rather be known as "the expert who helps women discover themselves," just as I have painfully done myself.

It was at that moment that I started a women's organization, called I AM WOMAN. It was to help women like me regain their self-esteem, rediscover themselves, and become the beautiful, sensitive, and powerful people they already were.

At last, I had found my "calling," just like the chief in the Outback said I would...when the time was right.

My "calling" was not being in the limelight, as I once thought it would be, but in being a fully experienced role model for women who were like I used to be: lost and empty.

But they need not go through all the bad I went through to appreciate the good. Women can learn from my mistakes so that they don't have to make the same mistake over and over again, like I did.

We are ALL beautiful, strong children of God. And, through full awareness and understanding, we can, together, rekindle the love, respect, self-esteem, dignity, and equality with men that our women ancestors worked so hard to gain back when Lilith left Adam in the Garden of Eden.

Preface

It all started in a tropical paradise called the Garden of Eden. The creator of the universe made man in His image. At the same time and from the same earth, He created woman. He called the man Adam (which means "earth"). And the woman, he called Lilith (which means "of the night"). But right from the start, there was trouble in paradise.

Adam was a domineering and controlling man who wanted to rule over Lilith. But Lilith was a proud and willful woman who claimed equality with Adam. And so, she left the Garden of Eden in pursuit of her own independence.

God then created another woman for Adam. This woman, he called Eve. And this event was the beginning of woman's constant, endless struggle for equality with man.

That is what I AM WOMAN is all about.

God originally created man and woman to be equal and to live in peace and harmony with each other. But since the beginning of time, man has considered himself the superior sex. This was the beginning of the ego and pride and both man and woman's downfall.

History says that the first woman to take up her pen in defense of her sex was Christine de Pizan. This was back in the fourteenth century. By the nineteenth century, women had united to fight for inequalities, primarily on gaining women's suffrage. This crusade became known as the feminist movement (aka "women's lib" or "women's liberation").

The movement began in the Western world, and has gone through three waves.

The first wave was in the late 1800s. It was oriented around middle- and upper-class white women.

The second wave began in the 1960s. It addressed unofficial inequalities, sexuality, and perhaps most controversially, reproductive rights.

The third wave, which started in the 1980s and continues through the present, focused on embracing contradictions, conflict, and irrationality. It attempted to accommodate diversity and change.

Today, in the twenty-first century, the chains have been broken, thanks to women like Gloria Steinem, Betty Friedan, and Germaine Greer.

It is time to make amends for Lilith and all the women who have been fighting for equality throughout the centuries.

I AM WOMAN is the fourth wave in the feminist movement. Here, women are seeking to gain empowerment and reinvent themselves and, finally, to reach equality between the sexes, thereby reuniting men and women as ONE, in love and with harmony, just as God intended in the beginning.

Finally, women can break out of the cocoons in which they have hidden across the ocean of time, and evolve into the lustrous, beautiful butterflies they were created to be.

I AM WOMAN will validate what our female ancestors laboriously worked for: freedom and equality.

We are in a period of wondrous evolution. I AM WOMAN may someday be written in the history books as the "fourth wave" in the feminist movement: the tsunami and final wave, when men and women are finally reunited and women can stand tall and find their rightful place in society.

Chapter 1

The Beginning

In the Merriam-Webster dictionary, *feminism* is described as "the theory of the political, economic and social equality of the sexes." However, the history of women has been one of submission.

There was no getting out of it and no divorce. You were stuck 'til death do you part: no matter how abusive or cruel.

The feminist movement began in the late eighteenth century in the United Kingdom and the United States. It has gone through three "waves."

The first wave was initiated in the nineteenth century and lasted until the twenty-first century.

It began in 1848 with the seventy-year fight for the women's right to vote. It began over tea.

It was on July 13, in the year 1848, that a New York housewife named Elizabeth Cady Stanton had friends over to discuss her discontent with the limitations placed on women's situations under America's so-called democracy.

Within a few days, these women picked a date for the convention. Its basis was to discuss social, civil, and religious conditions, and especially all rights for women. The gathering took place in Seneca Falls, New York, on July 19 and 20, 1848.

Among the topics discussed were the following:

1) Married women were legally "dead" in the eyes of the law.
2) Women were not allowed to vote.
3) Married women had no property rights.
4) Husbands had legal power over women and responsibility for their wives to the extent that they could imprison or beat them.
5) Women were not allowed to enter professional fields such as law or medicine.

6) Women were not allowed to participate in the affairs of the church.
7) Women were robbed of their self-confidence and self-respect, and were totally dependent on men.

The convention was convened. Then, two days later, a document called the Declaration of Sentiments and twelve resolutions received unanimous endorsements.

Let's take off our hats to these courageous women for standing up for what they believed was right. Little did they know that they started a movement that would continue for centuries.

Margaret Meade got it right when she said, "Never doubt that a small group of thoughtful, committed and fully focused citizens, with a common lofty dream, can change the world."

And indeed, only collective dreaming, shared by a few focused and passionate people, has ever changed the world.

Unfortunately, as the years of fighting for equality crept toward victory, relationships between men and women slowly deteriorated.

That's because when most men hear the words *women's lib,* they frown and grimace. You see, most men think *women's lib* means that women should wear the pants and be less feminine. They also think it will mean an end to their relationship or divorce. WRONG!

Much of this distorted impression has been caused by women themselves, and unless women take responsibility for having helped create it, they will have no power to change it.

In truth, women's lib is an awareness program that has educated women about themselves. And, it was through this program that women began to set aside their doubts and place a higher value on themselves. Unfortunately, it did not include men.

It has been forty years since Gloria Steinem said, "Women's liberation aims to not only free women but men as well." She went on to say, "Women are sisters, just like men are brothers. They have many of the very same problems. And, unlike men, they communicate with each other. The women's movement is a very important revolutionary and communication bridge, which we are building" (Wikipedia.org).

It has been nearly 300 years since the onslaught of the fight for equality and it's still lingering on. It has still not fully embraced men. But with this clearer understanding of where the women's lib movement went wrong, we are erecting a bridge of equality that finally brings men and women together as ONE. This unification organization is called, I AM WOMAN.

I AM WOMAN is the "fourth wave" and ideally the last one. Finally, equality will be reached on all issues and men and women will reunite as co-independents instead of co-dependents. And this "at-one-ment" will finally be through love, understanding, equality, and freedom.

Chapter 2

The Second Wave in the Movement

What did Twiggy, The Beatles, miniskirts, hippies, and the women's liberation movement have in common?

They were all icons of the sixties: the era of pot smoking, the introduction of miniskirts, The Beatles and the "British invasion" of American music, and women ... still striving for equality.

Bouffant hairstyles and pillbox hats were the rage. Women were thought of as ornaments, with their place in the home.

Along with the many life-altering changes that this era brought, the "second wave" of the feminist movement began. It represented a seemingly abrupt break with the tranquil suburban life pictured in American popular culture.

Rape crisis centers were established.

Children's books were written that challenged sexual stereotypes.

Having been excluded from male-dominated occupations for decades, women finally found jobs as doctors, lawyers, pilots, construction workers, soldiers, bankers, and bus drivers.

Unlike the first wave, the second wave provoked extensive theoretical discussion about the origins of women's oppression, the nature of gender, and women's role in the family.

Women fought to liberate themselves from the traditional roles of wife and mother. Iconic images such as bra burning made women's lib a powerful movement.

But, the "bra burning" story was just a false rumor started by a woman as a way of imprinting a message to the public.

A woman from a small town in Ohio made a huge impact on the second wave in women's lib. Her name was Gloria Marie Steinem, and she was a political activist who became recognized as a leader of the women's liberation movement.

Steinem actively campaigned for the Equal Rights Amendment, in addition to other laws that promoted equality between men and women, and against discriminatory laws such as those that gave men superior rights in marriage.

In 1960, Playboy opened its first much-touted Playboy Club, which was called a rebellion against domesticity. It honored the "cool" bachelor, who drank martinis and had a line of Playmates who were too willing to "give it up" without a commitment.

In 1965, a "girlie" magazine for men called *Penthouse* accompanied *Playboy* magazine in promoting sexually explicit pictorials of women they dubbed "the girl next door."

Women fought for their right not to be symbolized as "beauty objects" or "sex objects." In fact in 1968, 100 women protested the Miss America Pageant because it promoted physical attractiveness and charm as the primary measures of a woman's worth.

It was a decade later that women launched the first magazine for women, where men would pose similar to the women who posed for *Playboy.* Many men objected to *Playgirl,* saying that it was only for gay men. But what's good for the goose is also good for the gander! Equal rights means exploiting men as well as women. Correct?

And so, the battle for power between men and women's superiority began.

One important feminist goal during this wave was to get women to run for office. Today women have been elected president in countries such as Israel, Argentina, Costa Rica, Iceland, Malta, and the Philippines.

For obvious reasons, men felt threatened by the women's liberation movement. To them, it represented opposition to the traditional training they underwent, such as the idea that "women should be barefoot and pregnant" and "a woman's place is in the kitchen and in the bedroom."

They believed that women's lib meant an end to their

relationships with women. In many cases, it did. And that is where women's lib went wrong.

Women's lib was created to be a "woman's awareness program" that educated women about themselves. Through this process, women began to set aside their doubts and place a higher value on themselves. And, by the end of the first wave, women had climbed one-quarter up the "ladder of equality." But still the power battle raged on between men and women.

It was forty years ago that women's rights advocate Gloria Steinem said, "Women's liberation aims to free men, too." (But, did it?)

"Women are sisters," she said. "We have many of the same problems and we communicate with one another. The women's lib movement is an important revolutionary bridge and we are continually building it" (wikipedia.org).

Centuries later, there is still a bit of women's oppression, and the fight for equality and the bridge of equality have also separated men and women more and more. And so it is that the era of the fourth wave, the final wave, was created. It is called I AM WOMAN. Through this wave, we hope to eliminate all of women's oppression once and for all and finally reach total equality with men in every area of endeavor.

It is our mission to finally reunite man and woman as ONE, just as God intended in the beginning.

Chapter 3

The Third Wave

Conflicts like when President Clinton changed the meaning of oral sex, saying it wasn't sex at all: and, when Anita Hill accused Clarence Thomas (a man who had been nominated to the U.S. Supreme Court) of sexual harassment. For those of you who don't know the outcome, our U.S. Senate voted 52-48 in favor of Thomas's nomination.

These and other tensions have affected changes in our society, including the no-fault divorce, women's rights to make decisions about pregnancy, abortion, and the right to own property.

The third-wave feminists are often proponents of using nonsexist language, using *Ms.* to refer to both married and unmarried women.

Many women who marry today choose to keep their maiden name instead of taking their husband's last name. This is a symbol of power and independence.

Childbearing out of wedlock has become more socially acceptable. In conservative Judaism, women can be ordained as rabbis. There are some Protestant women who are ordained as clergy.

Third-wave women come in all sizes, shapes, and flavors. They are career women, mothers, wives, lovers, bitches, sex symbols, activists, doctors, politicians, lesbians, and "girly girls."

In truth, the Third Wave was started to accommodate diversity and change. It is true that the Third wave is far from what the advocates of the first and second waves fought for. But, it is also true, that, through the efforts of the third wave, many positive changes have occurred.

Today, there are women in government, as well as women pursuing careers and raising children.

Third-wave feminism continues to be a substantial voice in America, and it continues to seek for the betterment for women across racial, class, and sexuality lines.

Furthermore, third-wave feminism has made great strides in reaching out to women in various nations, so that women from the so-called developing world can partake in a more transnational version of feminism. It is characterized by a desire of young women to find a voice of their own.

Now, because of the hard work that the feminists of the third wave have accomplished, women are *almost* at the top of the equality ladder.

Chapter 4

The Fourth Wave: I AM WOMAN

Feminism as a movement in America has now largely played itself out.

The work in America is *almost* done!

With the fourth and final wave, I AM WOMAN, the work that our ancestors have fought for centuries to achieve will almost be accomplished.

It is clear that many of women's demands have still not been met. However, with the coming of the organization I AM WOMAN, we have reason to be optimistic about the future.

The fourth wave will *not* be a continuation of the three previous waves. Instead, it will be the tsunami wave … the BIG ONE! Here, we will reunite men and women, just as they should have been reunited in the beginning. But this time, through co-independence not co-dependence.

At last, man and woman will be united in every way and on every level as co-equals and co-supporters—but through love and harmony, not dissension and disharmony.

Today, women throughout the world are elected to run countries. But we must remember that it took seventy years for American women to get the right to vote, and some even lost their lives for It!

More women have become the majority on college campuses and are getting better grades than men *(The New York Times)*.

Even the fight for equal pay is an argument about statistics. These, too, are the fruits of feminists' success and our need to take that "extra step."

The quest for equality has become a quest not only for American women but is NOW being pursued by women in every corner of the planet. And this is proving that this once, seemingly, impossible dream is, indeed, POSSIBLE!

Anywhere that women are still lagging behind men, I AM WOMAN will be there!

I AM WOMAN will always be anywhere we need to be to protect, defend, and finalize every current and future right to which a woman is entitled, by her birthright and our Constitution, to pursue health, happiness, justice and freedom, which are our alienable rights.

"I Am Woman"

Soon to be released:
"The Butterfly Effect"

Part Two in the "I Am Woman" series.
Sequel to be released in Fall, 2011

For information on becoming a member:
www.iamwoman.us.com